Original title:
The Secret of the Sea Breeze

Copyright © 2025 Creative Arts Management OÜ
All rights reserved.

Author: Wyatt Kensington
ISBN HARDBACK: 978-1-80581-547-1
ISBN PAPERBACK: 978-1-80581-074-2
ISBN EBOOK: 978-1-80581-547-1

Journey of the Wandering Breeze

A gust that tickles seashell ears,
Whispers of laughter, not of fears.
Playing tag with flying kites,
Twisting tales of endless flights.

It tickles fish and lifts the spray,
Turns dull afternoons to a play.
Crabs dance sideways, crabs rejoice,
As the wind finds its merry voice.

Surprises Caught in Driftwood Whirls

Driftwood giants start to grin,
As waves bring tales from within.
A rubber duck floats past with style,
Winking as it goes a mile.

Sandcastles are squashed with delight,
By playful winds in sheer excitement.
Seagulls laugh at feathery friends,
While driftwood messages never end.

Tides of Thought and Whispers

In a tide pool, thoughts do swirl,
With seaweed twists and a pearl.
Jellyfish wobble, share a grin,
As secrets of the sea begin.

What's that? A sock, caught in the tide!
Clownfish giggle while they hide.
An octopus mimics a show,
While the tide pulls thoughts to and fro.

Dreams Carried on Ocean Currents

Ocean dreams in ripples race,
Carried fast to a funny place.
A starfish wearing a tiny hat,
Contemplates a jelly donut spat.

Currents giggle, swirl and bounce,
Where turtles swim and wiggle their flounce.
They race with clouds, oh what a chase,
In the grand sea-swirled embrace.

Breezes that Hold Forgotten Tales

In a world where fish wear hats,
Seaweed dances with silly chats.
Crabs throw parties, quite a sight,
Skipping stones like stars at night.

Seagulls squawk in rhyme and cheer,
Telling tales of love and beer.
Mermaids giggle, flip their hair,
While pirates play truth or dare.

Fleeting Moments of Salt and Sun

Sunburns laugh with silly pride,
As waves march in like a goofy tide.
Sandy toes and iced cold drinks,
Seashells gossip, what do you think?

Kites get tangled, oh what a scene,
As kids chase dreams where the sea is green.
Laughter rings through the salty air,
A crab in shades gives quite the stare.

The Mysterious Language of Waters

Fish whisper secrets in fishy tones,
Turtles gossip about their bones.
Dolphins joke, they flip and twirl,
As anchors dance with a cheeky swirl.

Waves chuckle, crash on the shore,
Suggesting pranks ten times or more.
With every splash, there's giggly zest,
Even jellyfish can't resist the jest.

Hints of Adventure in Every Whiff

The breeze brings scent of fries and fun,
As beach balls bounce in the sun.
Every gust tells of daring quests,
With whispers of seagulls hosting fests.

Sandcastles wobble, a royal show,
While tide pools chuckle, putting on a glow.
Splashing waves tease with salty cheer,
Adventure beckons, come on, my dear!

Murmurs from the Depths

Fishes gossip beneath the waves,
Hiding tales that the ocean saves.
Whales share jokes, oh what a scene,
As crabs do stand-up, quite the routine.

The bubbles giggle with every pop,
As seaweed sways and the barnacles bop.
Anemones bounce with a vibrant cheer,
While dolphins dance, spreading laughter near.

Echoes of Tidal Dreams

Moonbeams shimmer on the playful foam,
As starfish plan a big dance at home.
Turtles wear shades and flip-flop style,
While jellyfish jiggle and smile all the while.

Crabs tell stories of treasure and grit,
About the one that got away, but they admit:
Their shovels are weak, and their tales not grand,
Yet laughter erupts in this merry band.

Secrets Carried on Salted Air

Seagulls squawk, sharing juicy tales,
Of lost sunglasses and fishy trails.
The breeze spins stories from far-off shores,
As beach balls bounce and splashing roars.

Sandcastles giggle, albeit a bit shy,
While kids compete for the best pie in the sky.
A hermit crab boasts of swift, sneaky ways,
As tides roll in, marking their playdays.

The Dance of Waves and Whispers

Waves waltz around in a foamy spree,
Whispering jokes to the rocks with glee.
Seashells chuckle in twisted delight,
Finding their rhythm as day turns to night.

Each splash is a punchline; each ripple a grin,
The ocean's alive with a whimsical spin.
Starfish flip flips, and surfboards glide,
As laughter echoes from tide to tide.

Veils of Mist at Dawn

In the shroud of morning's hue,
Seagulls play hide and seek so true.
They squawk and flap with eager grace,
While sailors grope in the fog's embrace.

A fishy scent they can't outsmart,
Yet lures them in with nature's art.
With nets in hand, they trip and dive,
The harbor's laughter keeps them alive.

Ocean's Lullaby: Unveiling Mysteries

The waves whisper secrets near and far,
Underneath the sun's bright star.
Crabs debate who's king of the tide,
While clams in shells try not to hide.

A starfish waves with five-fingered cheer,
"Oh, please sit down, the coast is clear!"
But the swimmers splash and yell in glee,
Chasing the wrigglers of the sea.

Caresses of the Coastal Wind

A gentle breeze begins to tease,
It tickles noses, brings us to knees.
Sandcastles crumble with a puff,
As kites soar high, the sky gets ruff!

Dolphins leap with a flip and a twist,
While umbrellas fly, it's pure, blissful mist.
The shoreline giggles, waves dance around,
And beach towels tumble—oh! What a sound!

Tales Told by Seaglass

In shards of green, tales come alive,
From bottles that washed ashore, they thrive.
A pirate's treasure, or so they boast,
An empty soda, they laugh the most.

"Next time," says red, "let's be a gem,
Not just a piece of this old mayhem!"
The sun sets low, and they all unite,
In stories of ships lost in the night.

Portents in the Salt Air

The gulls squawk jokes in the sky,
As fishermen laugh and deny.
With nets full of socks and old boots,
They dance like fish in discarded suits.

The waves tickle toes on the shore,
Shouting antics, always wanting more.
A crab wears a hat made of foam,
Inviting all to join in its home.

Celestial Dances in Currents

Bubbles pop like laughter's delight,
Nautical creatures join in the fight.
Octopuses twist in a waltz,
While sea turtles tease, giving false halts.

The stars shine bright, or maybe it's fish,
Splashing about like they own a dish.
Jellyfish jiggle, a slippery dance,
Unruly and loud, they take every chance.

Secrets Held in Driftwood's Embrace

Driftwood speaks with a rusty grin,
Sharing tales of the ocean's din.
A twisted log, a crab's new throne,
Laughing at sailors, so far from home.

Shells hold gossip from shores long past,
Of seaweed parties that never last.
With nudges and giggles, they share their plight,
In a world where the tides are a comical sight.

Beyond the Horizon's Gaze

Far out where the water meets light,
Frogs on surfboards take to flight.
They mock the waves, they jump and play,
While mermaids giggle, come out to sway.

A fish dons a monocle, oh what a sight,
Debating seaweed on all things right.
With bubbles as records, they dance and jive,
In this watery world, where all seem alive.

Whispers from the Ocean's Breath

A crab in a tux, takes a stroll by the bay,
He waves to a gull, who seems rather gay.
The fish toss their scales, just to catch some sun,
While dolphins are laughing, oh what silly fun!

Seagulls are gossiping, perched on a row,
Sharing fishy tales, in the ebb and flow.
The waves prance around, in a quirky ballet,
As the sun winks down, at the end of the day.

Dance of the Wind and Waves

The wind is a jester, with a whisk and a whoosh,
Tickling the waves, in a playful swoosh.
A clam claps along, to the rhythm so neat,
As seaweed does the twist, in the salty heat.

A sailor lost his hat, but it's now on a seagull,
Who dances like a pro, with a cheeky pull.
The lighthouse blinks bright, giving a wink of luck,
As fish throw a party, just a bit out of luck.

Echoes of Coastal Dreams

A turtle on a surfboard, catching a wave,
While the octopus plays, just a little brave.
The sunset's a painter, with colors so bright,
Even crabs get excited, vying for the light.

Sandcastles crumble, with giggles and moans,
Sardines throw a bash, with homey fish scones.
The whispers of tide, tease the shells on the shore,
While a gull steals a fry, oh, who could want more?

Serene Currents and Stardust

Stars twirl like dancers, on the ocean's face,
While a whale hums softly, in his own space.
A starfish claims wisdom, in its coral chair,
Charming all the seashells with tales to share.

Mermen are bartering, for glittering shells,
As crabs tell tall tales, of underwater dwells.
The moon pulls the waves, like a playful tease,
While the sea laughs aloud, in a salty breeze.

Canvas of Colors in the Sea's Breath

When the tides tickle the beach,
Crabs dance like they're on stage,
A clownfish in a top hat,
Quite the theatrical age.

The seagulls gossip and squawk,
They steal fries from your hand,
With a twirl, they take off,
In a pirate's grand band.

Sandcastles crumble with glee,
While kids giggle and shout,
Towers lean like old men,
Just trying to figure it out.

A dolphin makes a fine joke,
Splashing water with flair,
While sea turtles just roll their eyes,
Like they haven't a care.

Hues of Light among the Waves

Sunlight pours like syrup,
Over jellyfish afloat,
They glide with no hurry,
In their transparent coat.

A clam's got a secret plan,
Closed tight like a vault,
But they can't hide giggles,
When the splash is their fault.

The surf sings a bubbly tune,
While surfers make a fuss,
One falls off with a splash,
Who knew waves could be so brusque?

Crabs hold a dance-off tonight,
With shells shining so bright,
Each step a ticklish flop,
As they boogie in moonlight.

The Tranquil Lure of Ocean Zephyrs

Waves whisper in curly wisps,
With a tickle on your nose,
The ocean brings sweet laughter,
Where nobody ever knows.

Seashells wear silly hats,
On a treasure-hunting spree,
With the waves as their bouncers,
They're the liveliest bunch, you see!

Sand dollars throw a party,
In the moonlight's glinting spell,
While starfish take the dance floor,
Their groovy moves do tell.

The breeze holds secrets so light,
That tickle and tease the mind,
Like a playful little ghost,
Leaving giggles behind.

Whirlwind Tales in Soft Breezes

The breeze blows in silly shapes,
With whispers for the brave,
Seagulls play hopscotch on clouds,
In a wild, feathered wave.

Octopuses with top hats,
Throw a tea party at sea,
They sip with their eight arms,
It's quite the sight to see!

As driftwood tells its own yarn,
Of times it fought the tide,
And how it surfed on laughter,
With sea creatures by its side.

The fisherman's rod wiggles,
As fish comically leap,
Each splash is a chuckle,
In this ocean of deep.

Enigma Beneath the Foamy Surface

Waves giggle as they dance on sand,
Fish wear sunglasses, looking quite grand.
Seagulls squawk jokes in the salty spray,
While crabs moonwalk, stealing the day.

A turtle tells tales of his race with fate,
Kicking up bubbles that laugh and create.
Starfish hold meetings on sunlit rocks,
Debating the best way to wear their socks.

Underwater, an octopus draws a map,
To find all the treasures and maybe a clap.
A clam snickers softly, just keeping it cool,
As jellyfish boogie, in oceanic school.

So here in the depths, where mysteries hide,
The craziest antics of fish coincide.
If you listen close, there's more to be found,
In waves of laughter, the ocean's sound.

Breezy Confidences

Whispers of wind tell tales so spry,
Seashells exchange secrets with the sky.
A dolphin laughs as it flips and spins,
While crabs gossip about who really wins.

The breeze carries stories of suns and moons,
Of picnic lunches and sandy tycoons.
Seagulls chuckle over stolen fries,
While beach balls bounce, caught by surprise.

A sunburnt pirate with a parrot in tow,
Swaps tall tales of treasure as the tides flow.
"Yo-ho!" calls the bird, "Don't be such a pest,
The riches are hidden under the crest!"

So listen well to the breezy songs,
They sing of fun where everyone belongs.
In every gust, a laugh floats free,
Mirth behind each curve of the sea.

Currents of Unspoken Stories

Sandy toes tap to a hidden beat,
Fish flip-flop along, with a twist and a tweet.
Silent laughter echoes in gentle swells,
As seashells gossip with whimsical spells.

A starfish winks at the moonlight's glow,
While toddlers build castles, letting joy flow.
Bubble-blowers parade with enormous cheer,
As the ocean giggles, wanting to hear.

The currents swirl tales of days gone by,
Of pirates sailing to plunder the sky.
Dolphins flip through tales of yore,
Each splash is a story worth fighting for.

In the dance of the tides, there's more to unveil,
Of tickles and wiggles, and maritime tales.
Listen close, for the water's embrace,
Holds laughter and joy of the wild ocean race.

The Language of Shells

A conch murmurs, "What's the scoop today?"
While timid clams watch the crabs at play.
Seashells laugh in their clattering choir,
As tidal whispers float higher and higher.

"Did you hear about the mussel's big plans?"
"Not without my barnacle-taking a chance!"
The ocean floor buzzes with giggling delight,
As sea urchins dance under the pale moonlight.

Coral formations nod to the jest,
While seaweed sways, adding to the fest.
The fish in formation, all flash their fins,
As barnacles boast, "We're the true wins!"

So gather around for a shelly good time,
Join in the laughter, let your heart chime.
For beneath the waves, where the tales swell,
Lies humor and joy, in the language of shells.

Morning Mysteries in Ocean Breezes

A seagull squawked, it stole my hat,
I chased it down, oh where's that brat?
The waves all laughed while I looked mad,
I stepped in sand, it stuck like gnat.

A crab came by, he winked and waved,
I swear he danced, oh how he braved!
I tried to twirl but tripped on shells,
The ocean chuckled, I heard its bells.

With jellyfish floating like balloons,
I took a dive, singing silly tunes!
But floated back, a ship of fish,
I'd never thought they'd grant a wish.

So if you hear the waves conspire,
Just grab your surfboard, let's go admire!
For laughter hides where breezes blow,
And morning mysteries put on a show.

Enchanted Shores of the Wishful Heart

Upon the shore, I wrote my dreams,
A seagull swooped, ruining my schemes!
It dipped and darted, then stole my fries,
While beachgoers laughed at my surprised eyes.

I built a castle, grand and tall,
But the tide snuck in and started to crawl.
My moats turned puddles, the walls went splat!
The ocean grinned, 'Now how 'bout that?'

Mermaids giggled as I slipped and slid,
One offered help, but then she hid!
They winked and blew bubbles, oh what a tease,
I splashed them back; they giggled with ease.

So here I'll stay, with laughter long,
At enchanted shores, where all feels wrong.
With fishy friends and tales of mirth,
Who knew the sea held such great worth?

Lullabies of the Tidal Air

Whispers of sand tickle my ear,
While seagulls gossip without any fear.
The crabs take dance lessons, oh what a sight,
In this coastal comedy, everything's light.

The ocean waves wear a tutu so bright,
Splashing around in their frolicsome flight.
The starfish are hula dancing with glee,
While I giggle at fish that swim round a tree.

A jellyfish juggles, what a bold prank,
Trying to float while riding a plank.
The lobsters are laughing, quite full of cheer,
In this tidal theatre, there's nothing to fear.

As the sun sets down, it's a splashy parade,
A conch shell conductor, an ocean charade.
The curtain of twilight wraps up the show,
With claps from the waves as they ebb to and fro.

Veils of Mist and Memory

A foggy morning with whispers around,
The seagulls are plotting quite low to the ground.
Their plans go awry with each gust of air,
As they tumble and flail with comedic flair.

The shells tell tales of mermaids' late night,
Who danced near the shore till the first morning light.
But their flip-flop shoes were left by the tide,
Now they're lost, much to their mischief and pride.

Crabs in their top hats with canes in their claws,
Recite poems of love, while the ocean applauds.
But the waves keep crashing, an uncontrollable beat,
As the dancers lose rhythm and scuttle their feet.

So here's to the memories painted in mist,
Where laughter and whimsy can't possibly be missed.
The veil lifts at dawn, revealing the scene,
Of a comically magical marine routine.

Song of the Salted Skies

With each gust of wind, a tune fills the air,
As kites twist and twirl without any care.
The clouds in their hats, like marshmallows, float,
While fish in the waves attempt to emote.

The dolphins leap high, practicing ballet,
While the gulls add a chorus that's silly, hooray!
Their feathers are ruffled, they squawk with delight,
As the seafloor becomes a grand dance floor tonight.

In the salty skies, where the sun paints the hue,
The ocean joins in with a rhythmic "Wahoo!"
Swing your fins and claps, to the beat of the foam,
In this zany paradise, everyone feels home.

So let's raise a toast to this salty old song,
Where laughter and joy help the tides to be strong.
For in every splash, and each gleeful jest,
Is the essence of fun that we savor the best.

Murmurs Beneath the Riptide

Beneath the waves, there's a ticklish tale,
Of fish playing hide-and-seek without fail.
They dart and they dash, still giggling with cheer,
While crabs take a break with a pint of cold beer.

The octopus dreams of a career in art,
Creating grand paintings, it plays the fine part.
But its ink spills out in a glorious mess,
Leaving canvas and color in complete distress.

With whispers of laughter and calls from the sand,
The tide pulls them in, like a comical band.
Anemones dance while the sea cucumbers sing,
In this humorous world, of ocean's bling-bling.

So toss in your worries with seaweed confetti,
Join the jolly crew, things will get steamy, not sweaty.
For below the surface, where giggles reside,
The murmur of mirth is our joy and our pride.

Secrets in the Coastal Zephyr

The gulls are plotting in the sky,
With snacks in their talons, oh my!
They squawk and swoop, what a show,
While fishermen lose their hats in tow.

A crab in shades struts on the sand,
Exchanging jokes, it's quite grand!
With a pinch and a wink, he dances about,
This beach is wild, without a doubt!

The waves roll in with giggles and glee,
Tickling toes like a playful spree.
And when the tide pulls back with a sigh,
It leaves behind treasures to dry.

So raise your drinks to the breeze so bright,
That brings us laughter, day and night!
With secrets swirling in each gust,
We'll dance on the shores, that's a must!

Enchanted Shores and Wind's Caress

On sandy castles, seagulls peep,
While mermaids giggle and swim so deep.
A wave rides in, wearing a hat,
Splashes the beach, 'A snack!' it spat.

The wind whispers tales of days gone by,
Of pirates' chests and a turtle's cry.
With each gust a secret is swapped,
As fishy tales from mouths are plopped.

The tide dances back with mischievous flair,
Tugging at pants, like it just doesn't care!
And seashells laugh with a clink and clatter,
While surfers wipe out, it's all a matter!

Grab your flip flops, don't be shy,
Where laughter bubbles and seagulls fly!
In every swirl of the salty air,
Life's a party, if you dare!

Shadows on the Tidal Edge

Under the moonlight, shadows prance,
While crabs form a conga line, what a chance!
"Jump in!" calls a clam, with a wink so sly,
But watch your toes, or you may cry!

The water chuckles at all we do,
While silly dolphins perform their revue.
They flip and they flop, like they own the show,
And if you're not careful, they'll steal your row.

A jellyfish juggles with flair and style,
As beach balls ricochet for miles.
Shells peer in, enjoying the scene,
While starfish waltz like a royal queen!

Under the stars, what a dazzling sight,
Where shadows play tricks, and dreams take flight.
So let's gather 'round, sing loud and clear,
In this tidal world, let's share a cheer!

Embrace of Nautical Ghosts

At dawn the ghosts shake off the dew,
In pirate hats, a clever crew.
They giggle and dance on the shipwrecked sands,
With seaweed wigs and rubber bands.

One whispers secrets of treasure untold,
While another shows off his collection of gold.
With a hearty laugh and a soft-spoken hum,
They plot hilarious ways to have fun!

The ship's wheel spins, held tight by a shade,
Taking us on a whimsical raid.
Fishes twirl, as they fling a dart,
Chasing the ghosts, it's a watery art!

So toast to the spirits of yesteryear,
With salty air and a hearty cheer!
For in every wave, and every ghost's dance,
Lies the joy of our chance to prance!

Threads of Serenity in Blissful Breezes

In a boat that wobbles like jelly,
We chase the winds, oh so silly!
With a sandwich tossed to the fish,
They nibble while we dance and swish.

The seagulls squawk, they raise a fuss,
Demanding crumbs without a muss.
We laugh and shout, they dive and play,
What a fine, wacky, windy day!

The waves whisper secrets so strange,
While we wonder if they'll change.
With goofy grins and hats askew,
We sail on dreams in skies so blue.

The sun can't stop its radiant tease,
As we spin in circles, feeling the breeze.
With ice cream drips and sunscreen woes,
This joy, I tell you, nobody knows!

The Intimacy of Tides

Oh tide, you're such a flirty thing,
You pull us close, then make us swing.
With every wave, you bump and grind,
Our hearts do somersaults, intertwined.

While crabs do the cha-cha on the sand,
We giggle at their comical band.
Shells whisper tales of past romances,
While we imitate their funny dances.

The sun dips low in the ocean's bed,
Cucky in its glory, turning pink and red.
We chase the tide, we jump and yelp,
Can't resist the laughs, it's just ourselves!

Between the tides, we find a kick,
With sand in shoes, that's quite the trick!
Our footprints fade, but we stay bright,
Laughing under the moon's soft light.

Sights and Sounds of Lost Horizons

A horizon line, where dreams collide,
We spot a dolphin, oh what a ride!
It jumps and flips, a sea ballet,
While we gawk in awe, already sway.

The wind tickles our ears like a tease,
As we try to play it cool with ease.
But our hats go flying, what a sight,
Chasing after them with all our might!

Beach umbrellas dance like a waltz,
With clumsy legs and light results.
We clap along to nature's tune,
As crabs applaud beneath the moon.

With every splash, our spirits soar,
Collecting laughter, we'll ask for more.
So here we stand, forever bold,
In stories from the waves retold.

Ephemeral Moments in Glistening Gale

The gusty gales bring a tickle fight,
With hair gone wild, what a sight!
We leap like kids, carefree and spry,
As wind-whipped kites soar up high.

"Look at me!" we shout with glee,
While waves crash in, just wait and see.
A splash of water, a shout, a laugh,
We're all tangled up in nature's craft.

The beach is our stage, the sea's our song,
As we play along, where we belong.
With sand in our togs and smiles so wide,
In this glistening gale, we take our ride!

Moments we weave in the sunlit spree,
Like tiny gems from a sparkling sea.
With each playful breeze, we dance and cheer,
Creating joyful notes for all to hear!

The Play of Shadows on Pebbled Shores

Footprints linger where we tread,
While crabs dance, zigzag in our stead.
Seagulls squawk with a comic flair,
As we chase wind and flip our hair.

Boys toss shells like frisbees bright,
Girls squeal at gulls in daytime light.
Giggles echo with every fall,
As sand gets trapped in a beach ball.

Waves tease toes, a ticklish chase,
Sun-kissed laughter fills the space.
Breezy whispers call us near,
For silly games with no frontier.

With every wave, our spirits soar,
Life's a joke, we ask for more.
As shadows play on sunlit ground,
In this comedy, joy is found.

Harmonies Lost in Salt and Spray

Frothy waves sing a salty tune,
As fish jump, playing hide and swoon.
A sailor slips, does a funny waltz,
While onlookers laugh, without faults.

Beach balls fly like wild balloons,
Chasing the wind, like silly tunes.
Children drum with seashells in hand,
Creating beats that are quite unplanned.

A crab performs a jiggly dance,
While starfish watch, giving a glance.
Laughter dances in the spray,
As we all join the ocean's play.

The tide rolls in, like a playful tease,
Washing away our worries with ease.
We hum along, lost in our glee,
The symphony of the briny sea.

Revelations in the Wind's Caress

The wind whispers secrets, oh so sly,
Telling tales of fish who sprout wings and fly.
With every gust, a giggle blooms,
As fish and whales share amusing tunes.

A dolphin pokes its cheeky head,
Cracking jokes as we sit and dread.
Seagulls act as our judgmental crew,
Rolling their eyes at our crazy view.

Riding waves on a makeshift boat,
We paddle hard while the fish gloat.
Splashing water and yelps of delight,
It seems the ocean won't let us take flight.

In the breeze, laughter twirls and spins,
Each gust a reminder that fun always wins.
As sea and sky compose their jest,
We embrace the chaos, feeling blessed.

Rainbows and Whispers Beyond the Surf

Rainbows arc in skies so wide,
Which umbrella should we then decide?
One with polka dots? Stripes galore?
Each choice a chance for laughter to soar.

The surf beckons with splashing cheer,
We dive headfirst, fueled by no fear.
But jellyfish, in a wiggly fit,
Make us squeal, then quickly admit.

Sandcastles rise, like dreams afloat,
A royal throne for a crabby goat.
As we wave flags from our sandy mound,
A parade of giggles floats all around.

With wind whipping hair into a mess,
We twirl and spin, embracing the stress.
Each wave whispers, with playful ruse,
Come dance with us and spread the good news!

Currents of Hidden Pathways

In the foam of waves so bright,
A jellyfish took off in flight.
The seagulls laughed, they lost their way,
And thus began a hilarious day.

Shells were heard to giggle and squeak,
As crabs danced in shoes made of creek.
The starfish, too, joined in the fun,
Who knew the ocean could be this pun?

Gentle Secrets of Coastal Winds

The winds whispered tales of yore,
Of an octopus who ran a store.
He sold seaweed wraps and fishy fries,
But never caught the customers' eyes.

A dolphin tried to wear a hat,
But it slipped down and scared a cat.
The coast was filled with laughter bright,
At sea life antics, pure delight.

Serenade of the Unseen Voyage

Imagine a boat with a mind of its own,
Sailing in circles while the captain was blown.
The parrots squawked, 'This is quite mad!'
While fish rolled their eyes at the sight they had.

The mermaids had parties with crabs that could sing,
Celebrating all that the ocean would bring.
With bubbles as drinks and seaweed for snacks,
They danced through the night, ignoring the flacks.

Breezes that Whisper History

The breeze said, 'I once knew a whale,
Who thought he could fly, but just flopped and failed.'
His friends didn't stop with their jokes and their jive,
So he swam to new depths, seeking to thrive.

A crab named Larry wore bling just for fun,
But lost it all in a mad time of run.
The ocean echoed with chuckles and glee,
For antics like these were as fresh as can be.

The Essence of Forgotten Shores

Upon the sandy, sunny place,
Seagulls strut with silly grace.
They steal fries from unsuspecting hands,
While crabs do conga on the strands.

A beach ball pops, it's quite a sight,
A kid runs off with sheer delight.
But watch your hat, the wind is sly,
It steals away—oh me, oh my!

Buckets tip and sandcastles fall,
Amid the giggles, summer's call.
Sunscreen's slippery, a wild ride,
Slipping and sliding, what a tide!

Later, as the sun dips low,
A jellyfish makes a funny show.
It waves goodbye, then bounces back,
With a laugh, it joins the snack attack!

Dancing with the Wandering Air

Breezes whisper, twist and spin,
They make the kites dance with a grin.
A tumbleweed rolls down the street,
Chasing feet in a breezy beat.

Hats fly off with a poof and a laugh,
Mirroring tales of a silly gaffe.
Chasing after, a race begins,
Who knew the wind was full of wins?

A picnic blanket takes flight, oh dear!
Sandwiches vanish, no one near!
The laughter echoes, waves join in,
As seagulls join the joyful din.

With breezy bows and trumpet shells,
The air hums playful, electric spells.
Twirl and swirl beneath the moon,
It's a frolicking dance, a merry tune!

Breezy Encounters at Twilight

Twilight brings a golden glow,
As breezes play a cheeky show.
They fluff the hair and tickle noses,
While dancing with the blossomed roses.

An old dog chases shadows near,
While the wind whispers, "Have no fear!"
Butterflies flit with fancy grace,
Dodging the breeze with a funny face.

A fisherman tells fishy tales,
As the breeze snickers, pokes, and fails.
His net is empty, but spirits soar,
In laughter's arms, who could want more?

Stars start winking; the night does tease,
As the air conspiratorially agrees.
With every gust, a giggle slips,
Even the moon can't stifle its quips!

Tantalizing Hints from the Horizon

The horizon gleams with mischief's light,
As fish jump high in sheer delight.
Waves crash and giggle, a aquatic jest,
Each splash a chuckle, a watery fest.

A sunburned sailor hums a tune,
While crabs relay gossip in the afternoon.
They sneak around in their pinching way,
Chasing tourists who came to play.

Mystery scents float through the air,
Cotton candy meets salty flair.
The seagulls squawk with nasal tones,
Making every snicker feel like home.

Tales from Beyond the Surf

The fish they chat, oh what a sight,
They gossip about the waves at night.
A crab wears shoes, or so I hear,
'The ocean's a dance floor, my dear!'

Seagulls complain, 'No fish today!'
While dolphins surf in a playful way.
A seal just sneezed, and oh, what fun,
He made the big waves think they'd run!

Old sharks tell tales, with a toothy grin,
Of treasures and dreams, oh where to begin?
The tide rolls in with a chuckling sound,
While seaweed sways; it's circus-bound!

Octopus juggles pearls with flair,
While jellyfish float without a care.
Under the sun's bright, giggling beam,
The ocean's alive with a silvery dream!

Echoing the Silent Depths.

Down below where the bubbles giggle,
A clam with pearls starts to wiggle.
The eels dance wildly, take a bow,
While turtles ask, 'What's happening now?'

A shipwreck sighs, 'Oh what a mess!'
A treasure chest? Just my old dress!
The fishes drag it across the sand,
Laughing and splashing, what a band!

Whales sing songs that tip-toe high,
'No mermaids here? We're just too shy!'
A quiet dolphin starts to play,
Turns out he's just showing off, hooray!

In the depths, where shadows play,
An octopus dreams of a bright ballet.
Oh what a show beneath the tide,
Where laughter and secrets collide!

Whispers of the Ocean's Breath

A clam decided to share a tale,
Of how a fish once learned to sail.
With seaweed sails and starfish crew,
The ocean giggled, and off they flew!

Anemones bounce with every wave,
'We're the party, come on, be brave!'
Dolphins leap in a snappy trance,
While crabs join in for the dance!

The tide keeps time, a playful beat,
As every creature moves its feet.
Octopus plays the conch horn loud,
Drawing in all from the happy crowd!

Underneath, where whispers flow,
The sea's a theater, don't you know?
With laughter echoing all around,
The ocean's joy is truly profound!

Ebb and Flow of Hidden Currents

With every wave, the sea takes cheer,
A jellyfish shows off, 'Look here!'
The sea cucumbers giggle as they glide,
While a fish drags along a bright tide!

The crabs conspire, 'Let's paint the sand!'
With watercolors, it's simply grand.
A sea turtle laughs, 'I'll be the judge!'
As starfish smile and won't hold a grudge.

An echoing splash, the fun goes on,
The sea whispers secrets, till the break of dawn.
Coral reefs blush in the sun's glow,
In this watery realm, happiness flows!

As the currents swirl, and laughter swells,
The ocean's laughter, oh how it tells,
Of tales spun deep, with a playful twist,
In waves that bubble and moments missed!

Celestial Notes Beneath the Waves

A fish once sang a silly song,
With bubbles popping all night long.
The crabs joined in, a surprising blend,
They danced till dawn, what a fun trend!

The jellyfish wiggled with delight,
As the starfish tiptoed left and right.
A giddy whirl of fins and glee,
Underwater jam, just let it be!

An octopus played a ukulele,
While sea urchins cheered, oh so haphazardly.
With a wink and a flip, the fun grew bold,
As underwater tales began to unfold.

From reef to reef, the laughter soared,
Creatures united, no one ignored.
In the depths where giggles reign,
Oceanic joy is hard to contain!

The Promise of Uncharted Waters

A dolphin swam with a silly grin,
Teasing a sailor, 'Come jump in!'
The waves were high but spirits high-rise,
As sea turtles wore their best disguise.

With pirates who danced a jig on deck,
And mermaids giggling, what the heck!
Each wave a chance to play and shout,
In uncharted waters, there's no doubt!

A treasure chest filled with rubber ducks,
Brought laughter louder than clucking clucks.
As a gull squawked jokes from way up high,
The ocean echoed with a happy sigh.

With every splash, an adventure new,
Exploring the blue, just me and you.
So grab your map, let's set the pace,
For fun awaits in this watery space!

Secrets Engraved in Shells

On sandy shores where whispers hide,
Shells tell tales of the ocean's ride.
With laughter caught in every swirl,
Each secret shell spins a silly twirl.

A clam who dreamed of surfing fast,
Stored all the waves of the ocean's past.
While snails debated how to race,
In this wacky world, there's no sad face.

A conch shell boasted of wild reports,
Of fishy feasts and jellyfish sports.
With sandcastles rising like dreams at sea,
Every grain holds a giggle, you see!

As seagulls swoop and pirouette,
Life's mysteries pose no threat.
In shells we find, not just a spell,
But the joy of laughter all is well!

Winds of Change along Coastal Paths

The breeze blew in with a puff of cheer,
Whisking away worries, we had no fear.
As kites soared high with colors ablaze,
Children laughed loud in the sun's warm rays.

Old crabs strutted with swagger and pride,
Their sideways dance was a comical ride.
While gulls played tag in the salty air,
Creating a scene that was wonderfully rare.

Beach balls bounced and the sand flew high,
With a giggling group making castles fly.
In the midst of folly and fun galore,
Every moment cherished, who could ask for more?

So come, take a stroll along this shore,
Where laughter reigns, and spirits soar.
With every gust, adventures ignite,
In the winds of change, everything feels right!

In the Embrace of the Coastal Whisper

Down by the shore, where sand dunes giggle,
Seagulls squawk tales, and the tide starts to wiggle.
Shells gossip about the fish in a hurry,
While crabs dance around, all flustered and blurry.

A wave whispers softly, with a tickle and tease,
Telling tall tales carried on the breeze.
It nudges a sandcastle, makes it all wobbly,
Then rushes to shore with a laugh oh-so-robustly.

Buckets and spades, they stash secrets so grand,
With each scoop and toss, they create their own land.
The tide comes in, and much to their dread,
Their castle collapses, fluffiness spread.

Yet smiles persist where splashes abound,
Fingers in the sand, giggles are found.
For who wouldn't laugh at the ocean's sly game,
While the breeze whispers softly, "Who's to blame?"

Windswept Fables of the Deep

Under bright skies, where the winds like to play,
Fish pull their pranks, and dolphins pirouette all day.
A clam tells a tale of glories untold,
While seaweed giggles, getting tangled and rolled.

Sailboats are swaying, with laughter they sway,
Chasing the waves that want to get away.
The captain's got snacks, a feast for the crew,
But seagulls swoop down, each one yelling, "Boo!"

The squall starts a ruckus, like a big ol' joke,
And the fishermen chuckle, their nets all awoke.
For every big splash, there's a story behind,
Of octopus ballet and a whale out of line.

At sunset the surface, it sparkles like wine,
As waves share their laughter, in rhythm, divine.
They wink at the shore saying, "Come sail with me!"
With hopes high and giggles, on this whimsical sea.

Nautical Echoes of Forgotten Times

In the shanty of sailors, echoes bubble and chime,
With tales of old ships that sailed out of rhyme.
The anchor's a grumpy old bloke with a frown,
Who dreams of the days he was young and not brown.

The compass gets dizzy, making no sense,
Wandering in circles, a maritime suspense.
"North, south, or sideways?" it hollers with cheer,
While the maps just lie there, too bored to steer.

A parrot drops in, claiming he knows,
All the grand treasures and where the wind blows.
With feathers a-twitching, he fluffs up his pride,
As he spills tales of riches, with hardly a guide.

Anchors aweigh, all the laughter unfurls,
As sailors fall over, swallowed by swirls.
For when the past whispers through sails thick with dust,
It's bound to get funny and filled with good gust.

The Ocean's Gentle Serenade

Beneath starlit skies, the waves softly hum,
As crabs strut their stuff, all ready for fun.
The surf serenades with a soft swish and swirl,
As sandcastles grin, in a sandy swirl.

With a splash and a dash, the fish poke their heads,
Tickled by laughter, where the current treads.
A turtle named Timmy takes his sweet time,
Singing to the waves in a lullaby rhyme.

In the moonlight's embrace, jellyfish glide,
Dreaming of parties where laughter won't hide.
As starfish sip lemonade in their shells,
The ocean's gentle call, it charmingly swells.

So gather, oh friends, near the surf's softest tune,
For each giggle and splash, make the night a boon.
With every wild story the tide sweeps away,
We find joy in the chaos, in our own whirligig play.

Unraveling the Heart of the Abyss

In the depths where fish wear hats,
And jellybeans float on velvet mats.
A crab with shades, he winks with flair,
Sipping seaweed tea, without a care.

Seahorses dance in bubble-ball gowns,
While octopuses play with polka-dot crowns.
The clams all gossip, they're quite the crew,
Underwater parties, oh, what a view!

Yet in these depths, a secret lies,
Of lost flip-flops and old french fries.
The echoes of laughter, a bubbly cheer,
Makes even the sharks feel a bit more near.

So dive right in, don your fins,
Join the underwater jovial din.
For every wave hides a tale so bright,
In the abyss, we laugh with delight.

Breaths of the Sea's Eternal Soul

The waves giggle softly, a ticklish swell,
As seagulls drop shells like pearls from their bell.
Starfish wink as they strut with grace,
No need for a mirror, they know their place.

The dolphins leap, like comedians they flip,
While plankton hold talent shows, don't let it slip!
Kraken sells snacks, his octopus hand,
Shares nachos and laughs with the fishy band.

With each splash and every glide,
The ocean breathes dreams; what a wild ride!
Mermaids chuckle as they braid seaweed,
In this watery realm, all hearts are freed.

So ride the tide and let it unveil,
The humor and whimsy in every detail.
For within the waves, joy swims so free,
Embracing the fun of our deep blue sea.

A Lightness Found in Seaside Resonance

The sun winks at seashells, playing shy,
As crabs set up a dance party, oh my!
Seasalt popcorn flies through the air,
While mermaids gossip without a care.

Each wave rolls in with a playful grin,
Giggles echo where the fun begins.
A fish in a bow tie sings out loud,
While dolphins frolic, gathering a crowd.

With starry-eyed shrimps, who laugh as they cheer,
The ocean's a stage, come lend an ear.
In this quirky realm, the laughter flows,
As the tide brings joy wherever it goes.

So catch the breeze, let your spirit fly,
Where silliness reigns and worries say bye.
Embrace every moment, let your heart dance,
As the seaside serenades you in romance.

Mysterious Shores of Untold Journeys

Beneath the stars, the sand giggles low,
As waves whisper secrets only they know.
Gummy worms wriggle, they swim in delight,
Chatting with crickets beneath the moonlight.

The turtles wear sneakers, they're out for a run,
While pelicans ponder who's having more fun.
Seashells keep tales of sunken ships,
And sea cucumbers plan synchronized flips.

The horizon grins, a mischievous sprite,
As sea foam erupts with pure delight.
With every ocean breeze, laughter ascends,
In these magical shores, where whimsy transcends.

So gather your stories, toss care to the breeze,
In the land of the tides, where laughter's a tease.
For on these shores, where the silly meets grace,
You'll find the spirit of fun in each trace.

Tales of Stardust and Seafoam

Under stars that twinkle bright,
Seagulls dance and take to flight.
Whispers carried, tales abound,
Sandy socks are lost, they're found.

Bubbles popping, laughter sounds,
A crab in shorts skips 'round the grounds.
The tide pulls back, then throws a fit,
Splashing all; we laugh, we sit.

The moon's a big old cheesy grin,
As jellyfish make a silly spin.
Sandcastles rise to touch the sky,
But one big wave—oh my, oh my!

Waves tickle toes, we jump and squeal,
Sandy treasures hide, oh what a deal!
Seashells sing with a giggling tone,
The night air hums; our hearts feel home.

Echoes of Solitude by the Shore

Footprints left in golden grains,
A lone starfish complains the pains.
Seagulls gossip, oh what a sight,
While crabs argue who's more polite.

The ocean grumbles, a long, loud sigh,
Whispers of waves that pass us by.
Umbrellas flip like they've lost a bet,
And seagulls laugh at our sunburned set.

With each splash, a joke is told,
As beachballs bounce and dreams unfold.
Turtles wear shades, oh so hip,
While jellybeans fare on a candy trip.

Seaweed dances, prancing around,
Caught in flipping flops on the ground.
Laughter echoes, joy's sweet rush,
For in our hearts, there's always hush.

The Nexus of Sky and Sea

Sky so blue, a canvas bright,
Clouds become pets, taking flight.
An octopus wearing a top hat,
Makes all the waves dance and chat.

Bubbles and giggles, oh what a blend,
A fish on roller skates takes a bend.
With every splash from a playful wave,
The shore holds stories that all crave.

Shells gossip like old pals from school,
Building castles, a wobbly stool.
The sunset paints with vibrant flair,
As we chase the breeze and lighten care.

Seagulls talk about the best dive,
To be a beach bum, oh how to thrive!
Tides swirl laughter, in a jest,
In the blend of blue, we live our best.

Breaths of the Ancient Waters

The ocean breathes with gentle ease,
Tickling toes on salty knees.
Dolphins giggle at the sand,
As crabs put on a marching band.

Old ships whisper tales of yore,
While waves play peek-a-boo on the shore.
A clownfish wears a tiny hat,
While whispers float like fluffy cat.

Seashells clink, a jingling tune,
Composing ballets under the moon.
The breeze teases with a playful grin,
As we dive into the joy within.

In the shallow, laughter rings,
Stories of fish and silly flings.
With every splash, the world feels new,
In the dance of water, joy ensues.

Chasing Shadows Along the Shore

Footprints dance on golden sand,
Seagulls scoff at our clumsy stand.
In the chase, we trip and fall,
Like rabbits at a carnival ball.

The tide rolls in, it pulls us near,
We chase shadows, laugh with cheer.
A crab scuttles, gives us a scare,
While we pretend we don't care!

Our kites are tangled in the breeze,
They soar and plummet with such ease.
We giggle as they take a dive,
Tangled in the bright blue sky.

"Is that a dolphin?" one of us shouts,
Turns out it's just a guy with doubts.
With laughter echoing in the air,
We run, we play, without a care.

A Symphony of Wind and Water

Listen close, the wind's a tease,
Whispering tales of salty breeze.
It twirls the waves like a dance so grand,
While sea foam sprinkles our sun-kissed land.

Each wave crashes with a mighty clap,
Like the snares in a rhythmic trap.
The ocean hums a silly tune,
While jellyfish waltz 'neath the moon.

A seagull struts, like it owns the place,
Wearing a feathered, comical face.
We cheer it on, like a crowd in awe,
"Go, funny bird! You deserve a law!"

With every splash, we burst in glee,
Playing along the watery spree.
Nature's orchestra, wild and free,
A joyful mix, just you and me.

The Unseen Rhythm of Waves

The waves taxi in, one by one,
Tickling toes, oh what fun!
They say, "Dismiss your worries, kid,"
As they splash us gently, never hid.

We dance like seaweed, wobbly and bold,
Our laughter shared, a sight to behold.
A flip-flop flies; oh what a sight!
Critters giggle at our plight.

Tides collide in a playful way,
Mocking us as we dive and sway.
Slippery rocks, oh what a tease,
We slip and slide like a minor breeze!

The sun sets low, painting hues anew,
We stroll, side by side, in this view.
With chortles echoing from the bay,
We forget the world, just here to play.

Glimmers of Light on Rippling Waters

The sun shines bright on bouncing waves,
Like diamonds dancing, oh how it braves.
We jump and splash with all our might,
Creating ripples, a goofy sight!

In the distance, a boat goes by,
Sailing slowly, with a sneaky sigh.
Its sails are flapping like a clumsy bird,
While we chuckle; it seems so absurd!

A fish pops up, then dives back down,
With a wink that turns our frowns to crowns.
"Fishy friends, come join the fun!"
But they play hide and seek, every one!

As the day fades, the stars start to gleam,
The water reflects our whimsical dream.
With giggles echoing into the night,
We bid farewell to the playful light.

Timeless Stories Blown by the Wind

A mermaid sings, quite out of tune,
To fish who dance under the moon.
With shells as hats and tails that swish,
They giggle at stars, each wink a wish.

A crab in boots prances with flair,
He challenges seagulls to a dare.
With every tumble, they roll and flop,
Laughter echoes, they'll never stop.

An octopus, juggling pearls with glee,
Sips seaweed juice, oh what a spree!
A jellyfish joins, glowing so bright,
Swirling like lanterns in the night.

And as the tide pulls back with a sigh,
The wind whispers tales, oh me, oh my!
Funny dreams drift, forever spun,
In a world where sea life is so much fun.

Reflections in Salty Exhalations

A dolphin's joke creates a wave,
As seagulls gather to misbehave.
With shells as props, they start to cheer,
Making light of crabs with a missing gear.

Starfish stand in rows, all a-pout,
Claiming they'd dance, but forgot the route.
A conch shell snickers, rolls on the sand,
While gulls giggle, a silly band.

Waves tease the shore, giggling soft,
Their whispers carrying, then scoff.
A barnacle stuck, grumbling low,
Sparks up a tale about long-ago.

In salty breaths, humor does bloom,
Sailing through tales from sea's busy room.
Laughter bounces on tides so spry,
With every splash, the jokes just fly!

Soft Harmonies of a Wandering Gale

The wind tickles seagrass, a soft serenade,
While crabs roll their eyes, all dressed up in jade.
A fish with a top hat, swaying with pride,
Claims he's the captain of this salty ride.

Gulls doing ballet, twirling on high,
Landlocks are giggling, oh my, oh my!
With every swoop, they dance and dive,
Such high-seas antics, they feel alive.

Fluffy clouds gather, to join the play,
Tickling the waves, in a frothy display.
A spiky potato, a sea urchin in wait,
Decides he'll make hats, oh isn't that great?

So sing, oh breeze, with laughter and cheer,
To the quirkiest characters we hold dear.
In the vast of blue, where giggles are found,
The music of nature twirls all around.

Captive Emotions in Ocean's Hair

A seaweed wizard, all tangled and green,
Casts spells that make fish do something obscene.
They flop and they flip, in hilarious arcs,
Creating a splash, just missing the sharks!

A crab wearing glasses, trying to read,
Claims he'll discover a new kind of seed.
But every time he peers, he gets lost in the tide,
Swiping at barnacles, so full of pride.

Pelicans shout, with a trumpet-like sound,
Filling the beach with laughter profound.
"Whatcha got there?" they chirp and they chime,
Only to find it's just sea foam this time.

But still they persist in their quest for delight,
In this whimsical play where the sea's always bright.
As whispers of water dance back to the shore,
Joy bubbles up, oh, who could ask for more!

www.ingramcontent.com/pod-product-compliance
Lightning Source LLC
Chambersburg PA
CBHW072128070526
44585CB00016B/1568